Norman Rockwell

Text by **Margaret Feinberg**

Simple Prayers of Hope

HARVEST HOUSE PUBLISHERS

EUGENE, OREGON

Simple Prayers of Hope
Text Copyright © 2005 by Margaret Feinberg
Published by Harvest House Publishers
Eugene, Oregon 97402

ISBN 0-7369-1517-6

The author, Margaret Feinberg, can be reached at P.O. Box 2981, Sitka, AK 99835, by emailing mafeinberg@juno.com, or visiting www.margaretfeinberg.com.

Artwork and Compilation of Artwork Copyright © 2005 The Norman Rockwell Family Entities. Reproduced by the permission of the Norman Rockwell Family Agency. All images, except the images on pages 11 and 22, appear courtesy of the Curtis Publishing Company. The images on pages 11 and 22 appear courtesy of the Norman Rockwell Art Collection Trust, The Norman Rockwell Museum at Stockbridge, Massachusetts.

Design and production by Koechel Peterson & Associates, Inc., Minneapolis, Minnesota.

Scripture quotations are from: the HOLY BIBLE, NEW INTERNATIONAL VERSON®. NIV®. Copyright © 1973, 1978, 1984 by the International Bible Society. Used by permission of Zondervan. All rights reserved; and The Message. Copyright © by Eugene H. Peterson 1993, 1994, 1995, 1996, 2000, 2001, 2002. Used by permission of NavPress Publishing Group.

Printed in Hong Kong

05 06 07 08 09 10 11 12 13 / NG / 10 9 8 7 6 5 4 3 2 1

Simple Prayers of Hope

A grandfather was walking through his yard
when he heard his granddaughter repeating the alphabet
in a tone of voice that sounded like a prayer.
He asked her what she was doing. The little girl explained:
"I'm praying, but I can't think of exactly the right words,
so I'm just saying all the letters,
and God will put them together for me,
because He knows what I'm thinking."

CHARLES B. VAUGHAN

A Prayer of Provision

Prayer is faith passing into action.
RICHARD CECIL

Lois had been battling cancer. Miraculously, someone had provided her with the opportunity to attend a much-needed seminar. All the expenses had been covered, except for her plane flight home.

Sitting in her car, Lois needed $153.27 by 2 P.M. It was already 1:30. *"God will provide my need,"* she said confidently to herself. She leaned back in her seat and reflected on Matthew 17:27 that tells of the funds the disciples needed to pay their taxes.

"Dear Lord," Lois prayed. "I need a fish soon. Please show me where to find the lake."

Glancing in her rear-view mirror, she watched a black sports car pull into a nearby parking space. Lois recognized the driver as a woman from her luncheon group. She walked toward Lois' car and introduced herself.

"I know you don't know me very well and I hope you don't think I'm crazy," she said.

"I'm so embarrassed. Please don't be offended by this."

"What's the matter?" Lois asked.

"Several months ago God told me to put change in an envelope for you," she explained. "I've just carried it around and have been adding to it every day till I got the nerve to give it to you. I hope this isn't insulting. I just have to obey God."

Before she could respond, the woman was gone, and Lois was left holding an envelope with exactly $153.27.

Prayer is the contact of a living soul with God. In prayer, God stoops to kiss man, to bless man, and to aid in everything that God can devise or man can need.

E.M. BOUNDS

Prayers of Service

Every great movement of God can be traced to a kneeling figure.

D.L. MOODY

Born in 1910 in the capital of the Albanian republic of Macedonia, Agnes grew up going to church on a regular basis. Because her family lived next door to the church, they were involved in almost all the activities and events. Agnes joined the choir, attended catechism classes, and became an active participant in her youth organization. She also read and studied the lives of missionaries and famous church leaders.

When poor people came to Agnes' house asking for food, she watched her mother make sure they never left empty handed. Her mother would say, "Keep in mind that even those who are not our blood relatives, even if they are poor, are still our brethren."

Around the age of 18, Agnes felt a very clear calling during a time of prayer to pursue a religious vocation. Her heart was stirred for missionary work in India.

On January 6, 1929, she arrived in Calcutta, India. Two years later, while taking her temporary vows as a Sister of Our Lady in Loreto, she changed her baptismal name to Teresa. For more than half of a century, Mother Teresa served the poorest of the poor.

When asked about her work, she explained, "It would not be easy without an intense life of prayer and a spirit of sacrifice." Indeed, the effects of one woman's prayers have been felt around the world.

By day the Lord directs his love,
at night his song is with me—a prayer to the God of my life.

THE BOOK OF PSALMS

A Surprise Answer to Prayer

Prayer is friendship with God.

GEORGE BUTTRICK

Keith had found the love of his life, Laura, but he wasn't sure whether the timing was right to propose. God answered his prayers for wisdom in a most unusual way.

Keith owned a 1983 S10 Blazer. It was ten years old when he purchased it, and he had owned it for another nine years. Needless to say, it desperately needed some repairs. Even if he was going to find a buyer, Keith knew he needed to invest some time and money in the vehicle.

Over the course of a week, Keith managed to fix the problems with the starter and the four-wheel drive. But when he went to repair the passenger side seat belt, he discovered he would have to remove a large bolt he had been unable to loosen for years.

After lathering the bolt in WD-40 and a few good tugs, it finally came loose. He removed the plastic frame and noticed a diamond ring sitting on the panel. At first, Keith thought it was a piece of costume jewelry, but after a visit to a jeweler, he discovered it was a real diamond in a 14-karat setting. Keith had an engagement ring.

"I knew God was saying 'It's time!' " Keith recalls.

Two weeks later, he proposed to Laura. Since then, she has worn the ring as a sign of Keith's promise and God's faithful answer to prayer.

You had no sooner started your prayer when the answer was given.

THE BOOK OF DANIEL

Prayers of Hope

*Have you any days of fasting and prayer? Storm the throne of grace
and persevere therein, and mercy will come down.*

JOHN WESLEY

Clara Frasher lived in the small town of Gainseville, Texas. Each day, Clara watched hundreds of students walk into the high school that was located across the street. As she looked at their faces and the way they carried themselves, she felt a burden in her heart she couldn't shake.

"I don't know what I can do," she thought to herself. "But I pray that someone will rescue these kids."

Clara invited some other women she knew to meet and pray on Monday mornings for the students who attended the high school. These prayer meetings lasted for six years.

Within a few years, an unknown youth minister— Jim Rayburn—moved to Gainseville and accepted a position with a local church. His youth meetings— which reached many unchurched kids—were wildly successful.

Rayburn eventually felt led to start his own organization in 1941. Since then, Young Life has grown into an international organization that reaches more than one million teenagers annually through its ministry. Even to this day, the organization attributes much of its initial success to the faithful prayers of those women.

I pray to God—my life a prayer—and wait for what he'll say and do.

THE BOOK OF PSALMS

Healing Hands

The greatest gift we can give to one another is our prayers.

AUTHOR UNKNOWN

It all began with a knock on a stranger's door. A group of us from a local church were going door to door offering to pray and serve those in the neighborhood. A young child met us at the door of an older, rundown house and led us into the kitchen, where a woman had just received the news that her husband had died.

We apologized for intruding and humbly asked if there was anything we could do. "I've got a painful headache," she replied. "And I don't think there's anything you can do about that."

"Well, may we pray for you?" I courageously asked.

She agreed, and we tenderly placed our hands on her shoulders and head and began to pray for God's peace, comfort, and healing to flood her life.

Before we could say "Amen," the woman grabbed my hands and asked, "What's in your fingers? Are those magnets?"

I showed her my hands.

"Well, I'll be!" she exclaimed. "My headache is completely gone. Praise the Lord!"

We sat with the woman for some time, and later that evening we delivered some fresh groceries to her door.

I have prayed for many a headache, heartache, and healing since then, but none with the same immediate results. But on that day, God answered our prayers and filled us all with faith in Him.

He heals the heartbroken and bandages their wounds.

THE BOOK OF PSALMS

Faithful Prayers

It is not enough for the believer to begin to pray, nor to pray correctly; nor is it enough to continue for a time to pray. We must patiently, believingly continue in prayer until we obtain an answer.

GEORGE MUELLER

There's a story told of a young country girl, Bolette Hinederli, who was praying one day and had a picture of a man in a prison cell flood her mind. Along with the strange vision was a still, quiet voice that said, *"This man will share the same fate as other criminals if no one takes up the work of praying for him. Pray for him, and I will send him out to proclaim My praises."*

Though she had never met this man, Bolette prayed earnestly for months. And as she prayed, a faith rose up inside of her that one day she would meet him. She actively sorted through newspapers and magazines looking for his face. She listened to different people's stories and testimonies, hoping to hear something from their story that resembled this man's fate. But she heard nothing.

Sometime later, while visiting a distant city, Bolette heard that a former prisoner was scheduled to speak at a nearby church. She knew that the odds were slim, but she decided to attend the meeting anyway. She entered the small church and waited for the service to begin. After the introductions, the guest speaker walked to the pulpit, and Bolette recognized the man's face as the one for whom she had been praying.

14

We pray for silver, but God often gives us gold instead.

MARTIN LUTHER

A Building of Prayer

It is possible to move men, through God, by prayer alone.

HUDSON TAYLOR

A story is told of a group of believers in the Ukraine who wanted to build a church shortly after the fall of the Soviet Union. No longer under communist law, the people knew they were legally able to construct the building, but they still lacked the resources needed for such a costly project.

This determined group decided to build the church on an available piece of swampland. They filled in the entire bog with dirt—one wheelbarrow at a time. The land was finally ready for a foundation, but these humble believers didn't have anything with which to construct a building.

Eventually, government officials allowed them to take down an old, empty nuclear missile silo that had been built during the Cold War. As they were tearing apart the silo, one of the workers found a ragged, fragile piece of paper rolled tightly and tucked between the bricks.

It read, "These bricks were purchased to build a house of worship. But they were confiscated by the government to build a missile silo. May it please the Lord that these bricks will one day be used to build a house to His glory!"

The believers realized that God was using these bricks not only to answer their prayers for a new church building, but also as a delayed answer to another believer's hopeful prayer that had been written on a scrap of paper decades ago.

Never was a faithful prayer lost. Some prayers have a longer voyage than others, but then they return with their richer lading at last.

WILLIAM GURNALL

A Prayer for a Child

Prayer is reaching out after the unseen.
ANDREW MURRAY

Looking out on the T-Ball field, Gary knew that his son wasn't a first draft pick. He wasn't standing on the pitching mound. He wasn't wearing a catcher's mask. And he wasn't standing near one of the three bases. Little Leif was in outfield.

Gary knew that the better outfield players would be playing out in left field. After all, this was the area where most of the hitters for T-Ball would naturally hit.

But Gary saw his son—wearing his little pressed uniform—standing out in right field. He was in no man's land, the area where no one's ball ever goes.

His heart sank for his son, and he offered up one silent prayer: *"Dear God, could You please let my son catch just one ball?"*

Gary looked up as the next T-Ball batter took his swing. The ball ricocheted off the bat and headed into right field. Leif watched the ball coming toward him, but he was frozen. Forgetting how to catch correctly, the young child simply stuck out his hand, with the mitt facing downward, and watched the ball miraculously slip into his grasp.

To this day, Gary isn't sure who was more surprised about the catch—the coach, himself, or his son. But either way, one small prayer gave hope to all of them.

*Any concern too small to be turned into a prayer
is too small to be made into a burden.*

CORRIE TEN BOOM

A Prayer of Simplicity

Prayer—secret, fervent, believing
prayer—lies at the root of all personal godliness.

WILLIAM CAREY

In 1182, a young child named Francis was born to a wealthy merchant. The young lad spent years living a frivolous life, but several encounters with illness, a period of serving in the military and being imprisoned, and a growing awareness of the poor changed the course of his life.

While attending the church of San Damiano, Francis felt the Lord say to him, "Go, Francis, repair My falling house." So Francis sold goods from his father's supplies to pay for the repairs of the church. His father was furious and disowned him.

Francis decided to renounce all wealth and, as the

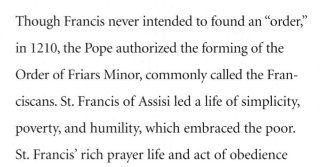

story goes, handed all his clothes to his father and walked away naked. He moved in with the priests of San Damiano and devoted himself to serving the poor. He worked as a day laborer for his meals rather than asking for money. Others joined him.

Though Francis never intended to found an "order," in 1210, the Pope authorized the forming of the Order of Friars Minor, commonly called the Franciscans. St. Francis of Assisi led a life of simplicity, poverty, and humility, which embraced the poor. St. Francis' rich prayer life and act of obedience became an example for generations to come.

There is none on earth that live such a life of joy and blessedness as those
that are acquainted with this heavenly conversation.

RICHARD BAXTER

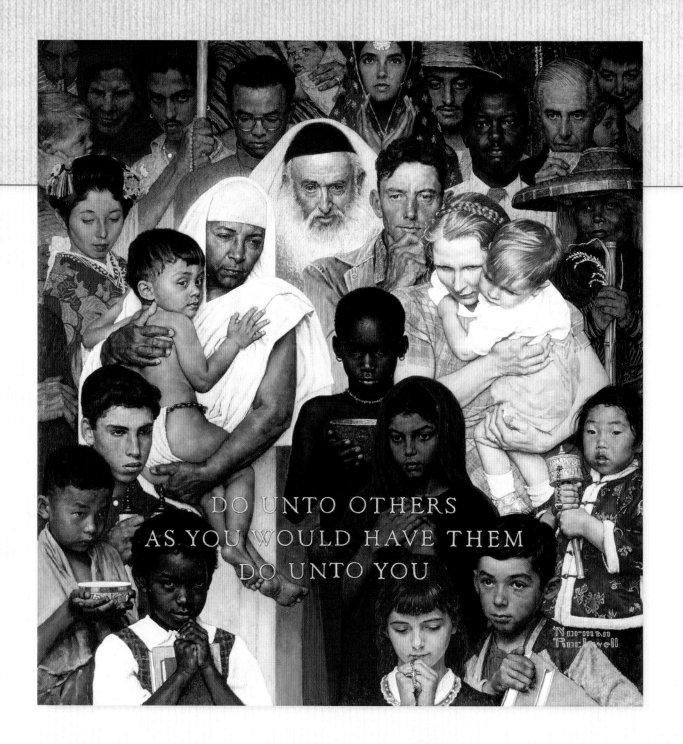

A Humble Prayer

Lord, make us instruments of your peace.

Where there is hatred, let us sow love;

where there is injury, pardon;

where there is discord, union;

where there is doubt, faith;

where there is despair, hope;

where there is darkness, light;

where there is sadness, joy.

Grant that we may not so much seek to be consoled as to console;

to be understood as to understand;

to be loved as to love.

For it is in giving that we receive;

it is in pardoning that we are pardoned;

and it is in dying that we are born to eternal life. Amen

PRAYER ATTRIBUTED TO ST. FRANCIS OF ASSISI

A Prayer of Mercy

The prayer closet is the arena which produces the overcomer.

PAUL E. BILLHEIMER

There is a story told about a rich plantation owner in Virginia. He had several slaves working for him. They were responsible for taking care of the land and his estate.

On a particular day, the wealthy landowner discovered one of his slaves reading his Bible. He immediately scolded the slave for neglecting his work; after all, Sunday provided more than enough time to sit around and read the Bible. To enforce his policy, he had the slave whipped and locked up in a shed.

When the slave owner passed by the shed some time later, he could hear the voice of the whipped slave. He walked closer and heard the slave's prayer, a humble plea for God to forgive the unfair and unjust actions of the slave owner. In his prayer, the black man asked that God not only to forgive his master, but that he "touch his heart, save him, and make him a good Christian."

The plantation owner felt the weight of his wrongdoing, turned to God, and became a Christian. One slave's simple prayer of hope changed the life and destiny of this man who owned him.

There is nothing that makes us love a man so much as praying for him.

WILLIAM LAW

The Power of Parents' Prayers

Faith is always praying. Prayer is always believing.

E.M. BOUNDS

Born in Barnsley, England, in 1832, James was the son of a Methodist minister. It wasn't easy, as anyone who has grown up as a preacher's son will tell you. But James' mother faithfully prayed that her son would become a believer.

As a teenager, James discovered a small pamphlet that told the story of one man's conversion. James decided to believe in Jesus and invited God to come into his heart.

Meanwhile, James' father had been praying for his son to serve in the mission field—China, specifically. James eventually studied medicine and theology in school before leaving for China to serve as a missionary in 1854—without knowing this was an answer to prayer.

Six years later, he returned to England with his new bride and spent several years translating the New Testament into a specific Chinese dialect. In 1866, James returned to China with 16 other missionaries and founded the China Inland Mission. In 1870 his wife and two of their children died of cholera, but James remained in China. Before his death in 1905, James Hudson Taylor established dozens of mission stations, brought more than 800 missionaries to the field, and became one of the most widely used missionaries in the history of China. It became apparent that his parents' simple prayers were more than answered.

Whatever else you are doing, so long as your heart desires God,
then you never cease to pray.

AUGUSTINE

Prayers of Protection

All I know is that when I pray, coincidences happen;
and when I don't pray, they don't happen.

DAN HAYES

A minister from Ohio once shared a personal testimony of God's protection during World War II. Stationed on a ship during the war, he and some of the other sailors would faithfully gather each day for a time of prayer. It wasn't always easy or convenient, but the soldiers knew of the importance of this prayer time. Together, they would ask God not only for personal protection but that the entire ship would be safe from the attacks of the enemy.

And God heard their prayers.

Time after time, the ship and its crewmembers were miraculously spared.

"In one battle, an enemy plane dropped a bomb onto the deck of our ship," he recalls. "Instead of exploding, however, to everyone's astonishment, the bomb bounced off the deck and into the water, just like a rubber ball would."

It was just one of the many times that this sailor–turned–pastor witnessed God's answer to their simple prayers of hope and protection.

Work as if everything depended upon work
and pray as if everything depended upon prayer.

WILLIAM BOOTH

A Son's Prayer

Prayer is wider than the world, deeper than the heart, and older than the origin of humanity, because prayer originates from the very character of God.

JAMES HOUSTON

Living in the small ranch town of Dundee, Texas, John Rice was only 14 when his father became seriously ill. A doctor had warned Mr. Rice that he needed to take some time off work to recover, but he refused and grew steadily worse.

The inevitable breakdown came, and both the family physician and the local doctor were called. Neither had any hope. John learned that his father wouldn't live until morning.

So John clung to the one truth he knew: God answers prayer. Though he had never heard a sermon or read an article about healing, he walked out to the barn, knelt in the horse stall, and began to pray.

When he came back to the house, he heard his stepmother praying and knew his sister had been praying as well. John had an assurance that the prayers were being answered.

The next morning, John's father opened his eyes, sat up in bed, and asked, "Where are my pants?"

Despite his wife's objections, he got up, dressed himself, and went into town. When he returned, the doctors finally got to examine him and marveled—he had been perfectly healed. The simple prayers of hope had been heard and answered, and a young boy's faith in prayer grew by leaps and bounds.

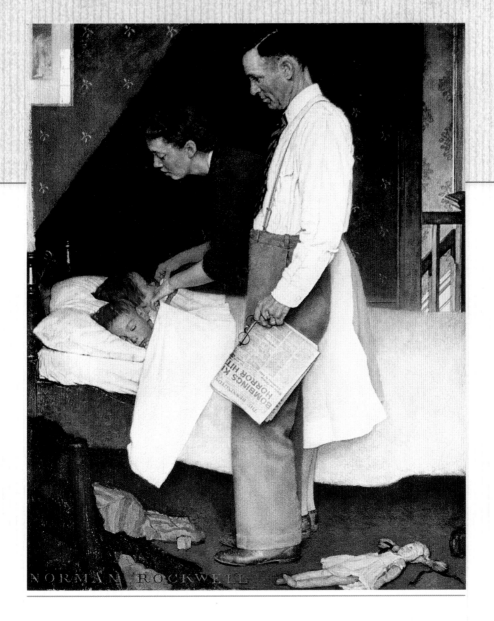

"Lord, teach us to pray."

THE BOOK OF LUKE

Notes

"A Prayer of Provision" contains quotes taken from "Divine Calculation" by Lois Spoon, *Today's Christian* (September/October 1999, Vol. 37, No. 5), p. 59.

"Prayers of Service" contains a quote taken from *Loving Jesus* by Mother Teresa. (Ann Arbor: Servant Publications, 1991), p. 139.

"Prayers of Hope" contains a quote taken from "An Adventure in Excellence," © Young Life 2003. Used with permission.

"Faithful Prayers" is adapted from *The Hour That Changes the World* by Dick Eastman (Grand Rapids: Baker Book House, 1978), pp. 71-72.

"A Building of Prayer" is adapted from *The God Who Hung on the Cross* by Dois I. Rosser Jr. and Ellen Vaughn (Grand Rapids: Zondervan, 2003), p. 140. Used with permission.

"A Prayer of Mercy" is adapted from *Sense and Nonsense About Prayer* by Lehman Strauss (Chicago: Moody Press, 1974), p. 49. Quote used with permission of publisher.

"Prayers of Protection" is adapted from *Intercessory Prayer* by Dutch Sheets (Ventura, CA: Regal Books, 1996), p. 82. Used with permission

"A Son's Prayer" is adapted from *Prayer: Asking and Receiving* by John R. Rice (Murpheesboro, TN: Sword of the Lord Publishers, 1972), p. 120.